The Seaside Switch

by KATHLEEN V. KUDLINSKI
illustrated by LINDY BURNETT

NORTHWORD
Minnetonka, Minnesota

The illustrations were created using gouache

The text and display type were set in Papyrus and Indy Italic

Composed in the United States of America

Designed by Lois A. Rainwater

Edited by Kristen McCurry

NorthWord

Books for Young Readers

11571 K-Tel Drive

Minnetonka, MN 55343

www.tnkidsbooks.com

Library of Congress Cataloging-in-Publication Data

Kudlinski, Kathleen V.

The seaside switch / by Kathleen V. Kudlinski ; illustrated by Lindy Burnett.

p. cm.

ISBN 978-1-55971-964-3 (hc)

1. Tidal flat ecology--Juvenile literature. 2. Tides--Juvenile literature. I. Burnett, Lindy, ill. II. Title.

QH541.5.S35K83 2007

577.69'9--dc22   2006011608

Printed in Singapore

10 9 8 7 6 5 4 3 2 1

To the National Park Rangers
who care for special seashores and landscapes so we all
can share these beautiful, wild places
—K.V.K.

To Gant Cookson, who generously enabled me to fly
to beautiful shorelines for the perfect reference
—L.B.

At low tide, low tide,
when the beach is wide and the waves are far,
sea creatures wait, dry and hungry.
Come and watch! Come and see!
The seaside switch is beginning.

Gulls flock and soar and dart and peck,
staying dry above the waves.
Listen! Waves crash and boom as the tide begins to rise,
pulled by the moon and the sun.

Clams wait in the sand
with their shells shut tight until…
curling, swirling, the tide rolls in.
Then the clams stretch their necks
up through the sand to sip seawater soup.

Seaweeds wait in a dark damp heap until…
creeping, seeping, the tide rolls in.
Then the weeds spread wide
to soak up watery sunshine.

Crabs scamper and scurry and poke and pinch,
finding their food where they can.
Feel it! Tidewater comes in cold as it rises,
pulled by the moon and the sun.

Mussels hang on their fine silky threads until…
crashing, splashing, the tide rolls in.
Then hungry mussels open their shells
to slurp the ocean stew.

Barnacles wait, stuck tight to the rocks until…
gushing, rushing, the tide rolls in.
Then they open to kick their legs
in the food-filled sea.

Fish dart and nibble and chase and flee,
swimming free in the salty waves.
Sniff! The ocean air smells clean when the tide rises,
pulled by the moon and the sun.

Snails hide in their shells
in the shadows until…
surging, submerging, the tide rolls in.
Then the snails slither out,
scouring food from the rocks.

Terns hover and fly and dive and fish
as they dip in the sea for a bite.
Taste! The rising tidewater
tastes salty and sharp,
pulled by the moon and the sun.

At high, high tide,
when the rocks are wet and the waves come near,
creatures feast under the water.
Come and watch! Come and see!
The seaside is switching again.

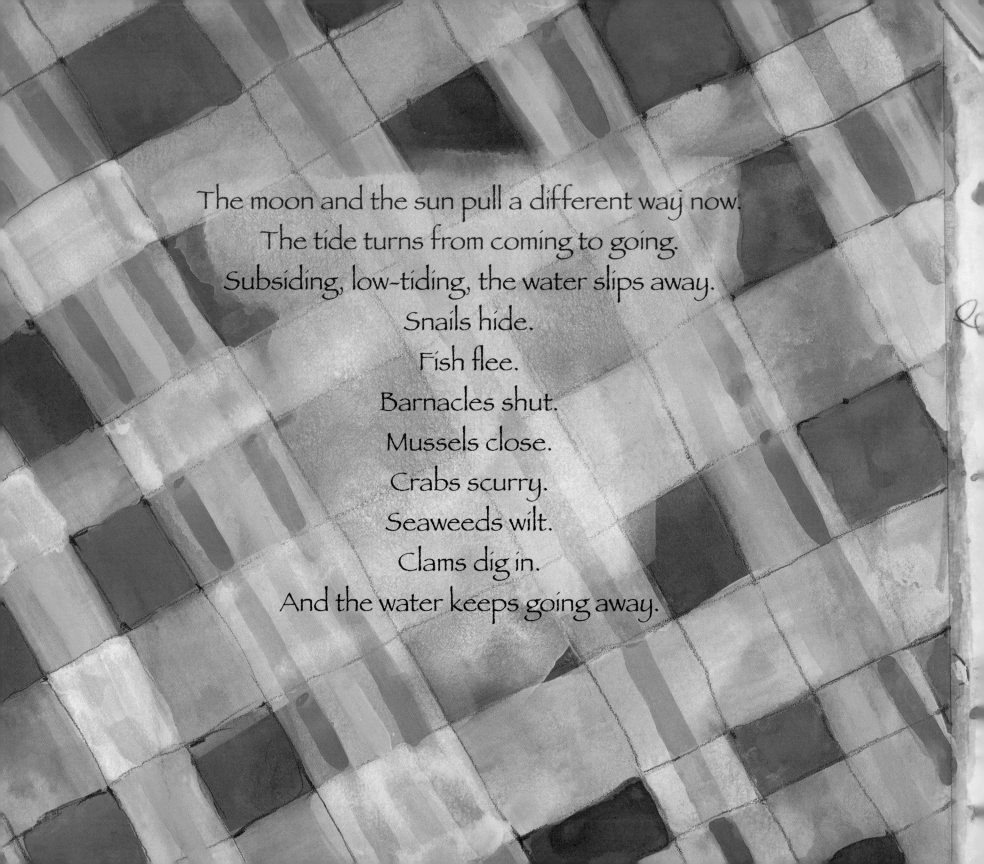

The moon and the sun pull a different way now.
The tide turns from coming to going.
Subsiding, low-tiding, the water slips away.

Snails hide.

Fish flee.

Barnacles shut.

Mussels close.

Crabs scurry.

Seaweeds wilt.

Clams dig in.

And the water keeps going away.

Watch! On the way down small creatures get caught
in tide pools made by the rocks.
They circle and chase and feed and wait
for another high tide to set them free.

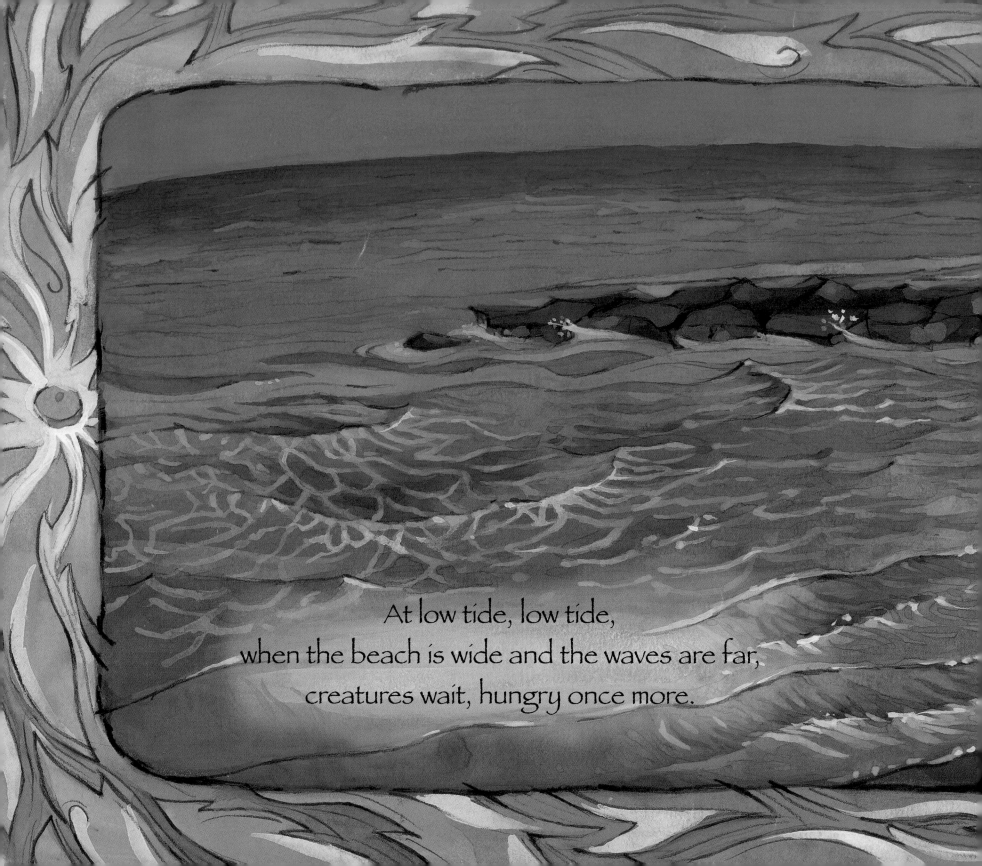

At low tide, low tide,
when the beach is wide and the waves are far,
creatures wait, hungry once more.

They know the tide will turn again.
As long as there's a moon and a sun,
the seaside tides will keep switching.

KATHLEEN KUDLINSKI has written more than thirty books for children. Every day she takes her sketchbook outside to the beaches, woods, or hills near her home in Guilford, Connecticut, or her cabin in Springfield, Vermont. See her sketches and newspaper articles on nature at www.ctcentral.com on Sundays or visit her web page at www.kudlinskibooks.com.

LINDY BURNETT illustrated this book after studying the seashore from Mexico to Maine. This sometimes meant balancing a sketchbook on a rock and floating in shallow water with a snorkel and a mask, studying barnacles, snails, and funny little fish. Lindy has won national awards for her work as an illustrator. *The Seaside Switch* is her fifth children's book. Eli, the boy who served as Lindy's model for this book, lives near her in Madison, Georgia, far from the ocean.

If you fall over, the Earth pulls you down. That pull is Earth's gravity at work. The moon has gravity, too. Moon gravity pulls at the mountains and oceans on Earth. Mountains can't move, but the oceans slosh around, pulled toward the moon. We call this movement high tide. Low tides come about six hours later, as the moon pulls the water to make a high tide somewhere else.
High tides do not always happen at the same time of day. That is because the moon takes more than a full day to swing around the earth. Tides have to follow the moon as it pokes along. The tides come about an hour later each day.
The sun has gravity too, but it is farther away. It does not pull as hard on the ocean as the moon does.
But when the moon and the sun pull in the same direction, we get a super high tide.